3|4

Intuition: The Sixth Sense

Clara Reade

PowerKiDS press

New York

Published in 2014 by The Rosen Publishing Group, Inc.
29 East 21st Street, New York, NY 10010

First Edition

Editor: Jennifer Way and Amelie von Zumbusch
Book Design: Kate Vlachos
Photo Research: Katie Stryker

Photo Credits: Cover Flying Colours Ltd/Digital Vision/Getty Images; p. 4 altanaka/Shutterstock.com; p. 7 Anastasia Shilova/Shutterstock.com; p. 8 kedrov/Shutterstock.com; pp, 11, 24 (uneasy) Pavel L Photo and Video/Shutterstock.com; p. 12 Andrew L/Shutterstock.com; pp. 15, 19 iStockphoto/Thinkstock; p. 16 Hemera/Thinkstock; p. 20 KidStock/Blend Images/Getty Images; p. 23 Fuse/Thinkstock; p. 24 (brain) leonello calvetti/Shutterstock.com; p. 24 (danger) Ryan McVay/Photodisc/Thinkstock.

Library of Congress Cataloging-in-Publication Data

Reade, Clara, author.
 Intuition : the sixth sense / by Clara Reade. — 1st ed.
     pages cm. — (Your five senses and your sixth sense)
 Includes index.
 ISBN 978-1-4777-2858-1 (library) — ISBN 978-1-4777-2951-9 (pbk.) —
ISBN 978-1-4777-3028-7 (6-pack)
 1. Intuition–Juvenile literature. I. Title.
 BF315.5.R425 2014
 153.4′4—dc23
                                    2013022437

Manufactured in the United States of America

CPSIA Compliance Information: Batch #W14PK3: For Further Information contact Rosen Publishing, New York, New York at 1-800-237-9932

CONTENTS

Intuition is a gut feeling. However, it mostly uses your **brain**.

People link it to the right side of the brain.

People call it the sixth sense. Hearing, sight, touch, taste, and smell are the other senses.

The word "intuition" comes from Latin.

Chokkan is the Japanese word for it.

It warns you if you are in **danger**.

If you feel **uneasy**, be careful!

It helps you tell right from wrong.

19

Ethics is the study of right and wrong.

What does your intuition
tell you?

WORDS TO KNOW

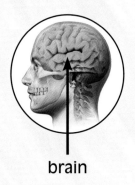

brain

danger

uneasy

WEBSITES

Due to the changing nature of Internet links, PowerKids Press has developed an online list of websites related to the subject of this book. This site is updated regularly. Please use this link to access the list:
www.powerkidslinks.com/yfsyss/intuit

INDEX